AVAILABLE NOW
from Lerner Publishing Services!

The *On the Hardwood* series:

Chicago Bulls
Dallas Mavericks
Los Angeles Clippers
Los Angeles Lakers
Miami HEAT
Minnesota Timberwolves
Oklahoma City Thunder
San Antonio Spurs

COMING SOON!

Additional titles in
the *On the Hardwood* series:

Boston Celtics
Brooklyn Nets
Houston Rockets
Indiana Pacers
New York Knicks
Philadelphia 76ers
Portland Trail Blazers
Utah Jazz

To Order • www.lernerbooks.com • 800-328-4929 • fax 800-332-1132

ON THE HARDWOOD

J.M. SKOGEN

On the Hardwood: Dallas Mavericks

MVP Books
2255 Calle Clara
La Jolla, CA 92037

MVP Books is an imprint of Book Buddy Digital Media, Inc., 42982 Osgood Road, Fremont, CA 94539

MVP Books publications may be purchased for
educational, business, or sales promotional use.

Cover and layout design by Jana Ramsay
Copyedited by Susan Sylvia
Photos by Getty Images

ISBN: 978-1-61570-513-9 (Library Binding)
ISBN: 978-1-61570-512-2 (Soft Cover)

TABLE OF CONTENTS

Chapter 1   A Second Chance   6

Chapter 2   The Beginning   14

Chapter 3   A New Decade, A New Game   22

Chapter 4   Almost There   30

Chapter 5   Champions   38

Chapter 1
A Second Chance

Dallas fans had turned American Airlines Center into a roaring flood of blue and white. This game was not just a regular home game—though it would have been hard to tell just by the sold-out crowd. After all, the Dallas Mavericks had a 9-year history of selling out each of their home games—an NBA record. But there was an explosive energy in the way the fans stood up and cheered their team on, a new kind of hope on their faces. This was Game 5 in the 2011 NBA Finals, and the Dallas Mavericks were losing to the Miami Heat, 100-97. The Mavericks and the Heat had each won two games so far in the series, but this was the last game that would be played in Dallas. Whoever won Game 5 would head to Miami

with a one-game lead and a huge advantage.

But American Airlines Center was also shadowed by the memory of another home game, in another Championship series. Five years earlier, the Mavs had finally reached

A Mavericks fan encourages her team with a picture of an NBA Championship ring.

the Finals for the first time in their team history. They had started that series off with a bang—winning the first two games. But after such a hopeful beginning, the Mavs were then crushed in the final four games—losing the deciding game on their own home court. And the team they had faced in 2006 was none other than the Miami Heat. Mavericks fans must have felt like they already knew how this story would play out—but they were hoping for a very different outcome this time around. They held up signs that read "Revenge for 2006," and filled the arena with their cheers.

The Mavericks were not a new franchise. In fact, the team was over 30 years old. In January of 2011, Forbes had even listed the Mavs as the 6th most valuable team in the NBA. But, in all of those years, the Mavs had never won a Championship. They had only made it to the Finals twice:

Mavericks Jason Terry and Devin Harris leave the court after the devastating 2006 loss to the Heat.

in 2006, and now in 2011. For fans screaming from the stands, they hoped that their team had almost reached the end of a very long journey. For players like power forward

Dirk Nowitzki has plenty of support from his fans.

Dirk Nowitzki, who had been a Maverick for the entire 12 years he had played in the NBA, every moment of his career had led up to this series.

It had been a very tight game all night, with players like Miami's LeBron James and Dwyane Wade closing the gap every time the Mavs gained a lead. Dwayne Wade had even suffered a hip injury, only to return later in the game. In the first eight minutes of the fourth quarter, Wade had put 10 points on the board for Miami. If this momentum continued, the Heat would surely head back to Miami with a victory. And so, near the end of the fourth quarter, fans didn't know whether

Rooting for Revenge

When it was clear that the Mavs might go to the 2011 NBA Finals, many Dallas fans began rooting for the Miami Heat. They wanted the Heat to win the Eastern Conference Finals so the Mavericks could finally have a chance at revenge for 2006.

they would leave the arena that much closer to being 2011 Champions, or that much closer to defeat. They cheered and banged their blue thundersticks together, urging their team to keep going. No matter what, Dallas was going to let their team know how much they believed in them.

With 3:30 remaining on the clock, the Mavs had just recovered the ball after a successful free throw by Miami's Chris Bosh. Jason "The JET" Terry had the ball and, coming in from the sidelines, made a quick pass to Dirk Nowitzki where he waited by the net. The Heat's defense rushed in to block what looked like a simple shot. Nowitzki planted his feet and raised his arms, like he was about to try for a jump shot. Then in the blink of an eye, he passed the ball through the gaping hole in

Jason "The JET" Terry does his signature move.

the defense—back to the now-open Terry. With the Heat now swarming around Nowitzki, there was no one to stop Terry from sending a rainbow through the air, sinking the 24-foot jump shot. The Mavs had tied the game.

Dallas did not let up. They watched for every opening—driving the ball past Miami's defense at each opportunity. The next time Nowitzki had the ball, he took off for the net. As he twisted his way past the Heat's defense, it would have shocked many to know that this blur of a basketball player was still recovering from a terrible sinus infection. He seemed to move in three different directions at once—one step ahead of the Heat. Then Nowitzki was in the air, slamming the ball into

Dirk Nowitzki takes a shot against the Heat.

Dressing for the Occasion

The Mavericks each wore at least one piece of black clothing when they traveled to Miami for Game 6. This was to show that they were going to the Heat's "funeral."

the net for another two points. The Mavs had finally taken the lead away from the Heat. Again and again the Mavs worked together to find holes in Miami's defense. The Mavs were not going to leave their home court without a fight.

With only 0:33 seconds left on the clock, the score was 105-101, Mavericks. Then, backed by deafening chants of "Beat the Heat! Beat the Heat!" Jason Terry reached

The Heat's LeBron James can't stop Jason Terry's jump shot.

12

up and over the outstretched hands of Miami's LeBron James and tried for a 26-foot three-pointer. Though it only took a moment for the ball to sail through the air, to the crowd at American Airlines Center it seemed an eternity before it swished through the net. Fans got to their feet, hands in the air, screaming for their team. They knew the Heat could not make up the seven-point difference.

The Dallas Mavericks would not have the massive blue and white crowds once they got to Miami, and they wouldn't have their familiar court. But they would be an entire game ahead of the Miami Heat, leading 3-2 in the series. And they would have this moment of triumph with the memory of their fans yelling "One more game! One

Tyson Chandler gives a victory fist pump after winning Game 5 of the 2011 Finals.

more game!" They would carry that encouragement with them for the entire 1,300 mile trip to Florida. In just one more game, the Dallas Mavericks might return to Texas as champions.

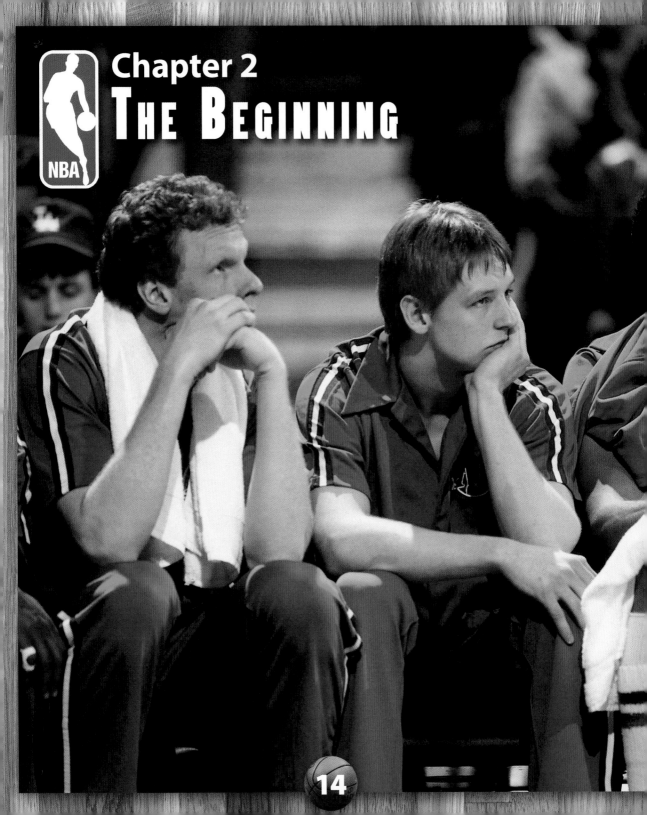

The Mavericks were not the first basketball team to play for Dallas. In fact, from 1967 to 1973 a team called the Dallas Chaparrals played in the American Basketball Association League. The ABA was created in 1967 to allow different areas of the country, that did not have access to the NBA, to enjoy their own basketball teams. However, in 1973, the Chaparrals were sold and moved to San Antonio, leaving Dallas without a team once again. When the ABA merged with the NBA in 1976, the Chaparrals stayed in San Antonio and became a team that is still very well known today: the San Antonio Spurs. But this merger of the two leagues still left Dallas without a basketball team.

Then in 1978, Norm Sonju, the

Changing Colors

Though the Mavs' uniforms are now usually blue on the road, their first uniforms were green with blue and white trim.

General Manager for the Buffalo Braves, announced that his team would move to Dallas. They were going to become the Dallas Express, named after a local railway center. Sonju had done a lot of research, and really thought that Dallas was ready and willing to have a new basketball team. When the Braves ended up moving to San Diego instead, Sonju didn't give up on Dallas. Instead, he started thinking about forming a brand new team.

Donald Carter, one of the richest men in Texas, had also decided that Dallas had waited long enough. He was determined to bring the NBA to

Dallas. Many years later, Carter would reveal the driving force behind his decision: "My wife, Linda Jo, is the basketball guru, and I was stupid enough to promise her a basketball team and had to keep that promise."

Donald Carter watches the 2006 NBA Finals.

With the help of his new business partner, Norm Sonju, Donald Carter kept that promise. Sonju went from business to business for half a year to raise the $12 million that they needed to buy a new team. Carter, with his huge Stetson hat and local charm, gave the financial security that helped convince investors to come aboard. In 1979, the NBA gave Carter and Sonju the green light. They could have their new basketball team for the 1980-81 season. Basketball was back in Dallas.

The year before, Sonju had wanted his team to be named the Dallas Express. However, he had only picked out that name for the Braves because, as he said at the time "I don't think we have time to run a contest for the public to pick a name." But now that they were creating their own team, and not in a hurry to move an existing one, they had plenty of time. The fans would decide the new team name. With the help of a local radio station, Carter and Sonju asked people to send in postcards with their favorite team name written on the back. The most popular name turned out to be the Mavericks. This may have been because one member of the team's ownership group was none other than actor James Garner. Garner had played the Wild West cardshark "Bret Maverick" in the wildly popular TV show, "Maverick." But they could have also liked that a maverick is the name for a lone cow, out on the range, who has wandered away from the herd. This word has come

Actor James Garner finds his inner "Maverick" during the World Series of Poker in 1996.

to mean someone who is strong-willed, and has a mind of his or her own: an independent thinker.

The Mavericks' first game of the official season was on October 11,

The Runners Up
The other two most popular names in the "Name the Team" contest were the Wranglers and the Express. All 41 people who wrote in "Mavericks" were given a pair of tickets to the opening game.

1980, and they played against the San Antonio Spurs. It seemed very fitting that the new Dallas team should begin its career by taking on the old Dallas Chaparrals. With the help of their new coach Dick Motta, and in their brand-new Reunion Arena, the Mavericks won their first Game 103-92. One sportscaster jokingly nicknamed the coach "Maestro Motta" for his big hand gestures during the game. He looked like he was directing an orchestra. And Coach Motta certainly brought out the best performances in his players for that first game.

However, after that first exciting win, the Mavericks went on to a very grim 15-67 record for their first season. This was not a promising start for the new franchise. But, with new acquisitions such as Brad Davis, Mark Aguirre and Rolando Blackman, the Mavericks began to improve as the years went on.

Rolando Blackman takes a shot against Los Angeles Lakers in a 1987 game.

By their fourth year, the Mavericks were consistent playoff contenders. So, though they had never won the Western Conference or become champions, people were gaining respect for the new franchise. The Mavs were becoming a competitive team, with a very promising future.

This positive track record continued until the 1990-91 season when, as though someone had just turned off a light switch, the Mavericks stopped winning. They did not have a winning season, and did not make it to the postseason, until 2000. This wasn't a great decade for Mavericks

Coach Dick Motta still knows how to "direct" the Mavericks during a 1995 game.

basketball. Looking back, there were many reasons why the team did so poorly for so many years. Many of the players had constant back and knee

Jason Kidd leaves the hardwood in a 1995 game against the Sacramento Kings.

of players, who came to be known as the "Three J's," took the court. Jason Kidd, Jim Jackson, and Jamal Mashburn brought a new life to the Mavericks' game. In the 1994-95 season, Kidd led the league for triple-doubles. A triple-double is not a kind of cheeseburger—a triple-double is when a player reaches double figures in three (triple) different statistical categories (points, rebounds, assists, steals, or blocked shots).

Jackson and Mashburn played like two parts of one machine. Several times that year, they both scored 50 points in a single game.

injuries. One player even had such personal issues that he was banned from the NBA for life. The Mavericks needed to rebuild and restructure a team that was truly crumbling.

Finally, in 1994, there was a ray of light in these dark years. A group

The Mavericks' win total jumped from 13 to 36 in a single year. This was a record for single-year improvement for the franchise. They still did not reach the postseason that year, but things were looking up. It would take five more years for the team to make it back to the playoffs, but some excitement and hope for the game was returning to Dallas.

However, when Don Carter sold the team to Ross Perot, Jr., in 1996, many fans felt like it was the end of an era. They wondered what they would do without their great Texan owner in the big white hat. Perot, however, only kept the team for four short years, and then sold it to another man with a personality almost as big as Texas itself: Mark Cuban, self-made billionaire. Fans,

once again, wondered what this new ownership would mean for their team. But, it would turn out, their imaginations couldn't begin to compare with what Cuban had planned for the Mavericks.

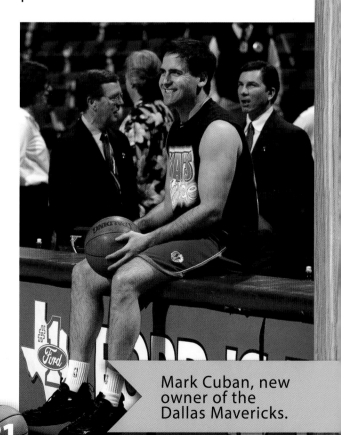

Mark Cuban, new owner of the Dallas Mavericks.

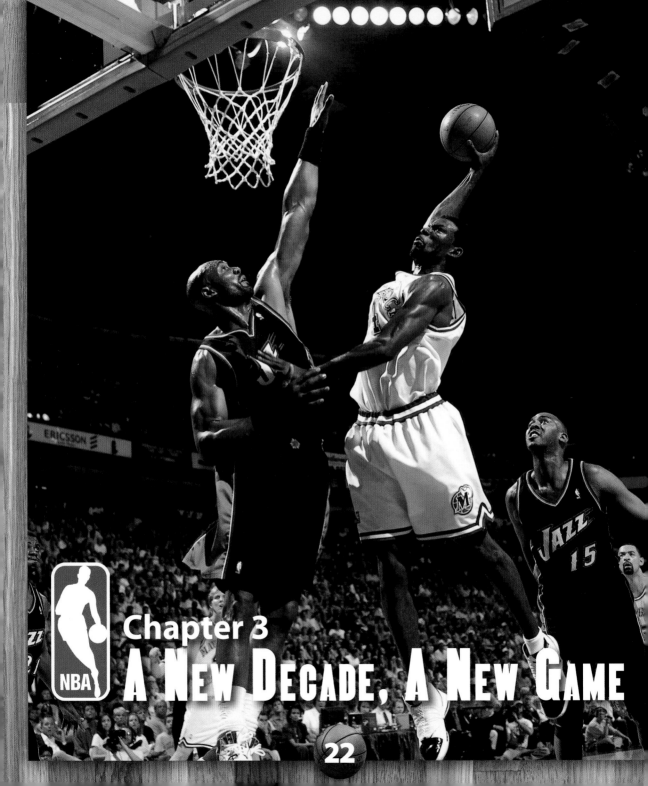

Chapter 3
A NEW DECADE, A NEW GAME

When the Mavericks heard that Ross Perot, Jr., had sold their team, they instantly recognized the name of the new owner. Many people, all over the country, had heard of Mark Cuban. Just a year earlier, in 1999, Cuban had made billions when he sold his company Broadcast.com to Yahoo.com. But the image of Mark Cuban that came to the players' minds was not just that of a very wealthy Dallas business-man. Instead, they thought of the noisy season ticket holder who sat near the court, yelling. Mark Cuban always came to the home games, and he always had something to say to the players, the coaches, and the referees.

At the time, Dirk Nowitzki had thought to himself "Ohhhh, no! That

Money Talks

Mark Cuban bought the Mavericks for $285 million. Even taking inflation into account, this makes the Mavs about nine times as valuable as when Don Carter and Norm Sonju paid the $12 million start-up fee in 1979.

dude!" Nowitzki, and many of the other players, wondered if this loud Mavs fan was about to turn their

Mark Cuban cheers on his team.

23

Nowitzki and his teammates received a fresh start after the sale of their team to Cuban.

lives upside down. They were right to worry. Mark Cuban had not bought a basketball team just to sit back and watch them play. As Cuban later said, "...I wasn't writing that big of a check just to stand around. It was a big investment, and I was going to do all I can to get the most out of it." But, luckily for the Mavericks, having

your life turned upside down is not always a bad thing.

Cuban first had the idea to buy the Mavericks after going to the opening game of the 1999-2000 season. The crowds were too quiet, and the game wasn't even sold out. Looking back on that day, Cuban remarked, "There was no energy in the building. I was like, you know what, I'm excited about this season. If I owned this team I could do a better job…" Right away Cuban took steps to buy the team. And, though Ross Perot, Jr., wasn't really looking to sell the team that year, Cuban didn't give up until the owner said yes.

Mark Cuban made many changes during his first year of ownership. For starters, he began pouring his own money into the team. There was a salary cap to limit to how much a team can pay its players. So, instead of writing the players a bigger paycheck, Cuban began to shower them with perks. He updated the players' locker room with personal flat screen TVs and video games. He bought his team a jet to fly them to away games, and even paid for them to stay in five-star hotels. Immediately, the Mavericks began to win more games on the road.

Not only did Mark Cuban give the players really nice things to play with in their off time, he made sure they had everything they needed on the court. Cuban hired more coaches, until

One of the Team

Mark Cuban tried to be around for all team practices, and would often play games of one-on-one or H.O.R.S.E. with the players.

there was a ratio of about one coach per player. This gave each player the attention and training to make sure they kept getting better and better. He also had the home games

The personal flat screen TVs and gaming systems make the Mavs' locker room a fun place to be.

Cuban (right) bought this Boeing 757 for the use of the Mavericks' travel.

catered. Both the Mavericks, and the opposing teams, were welcome to eat the healthy, good food. These details showed the players how much the Mavericks meant to Cuban. He was taking his investment very

Working Out at 35,000 Feet

Mark Cuban had a gym installed on the Mavs' jet, so his team could easily work out during long flights.

seriously, and he believed that they could be winners once again. These displays of generosity also showed the other teams in the NBA that it was good to be a Maverick. Other players, when their contracts were up, might think about heading over to Dallas.

Mark Cuban knew, however,

that the players were not the only people who mattered in a game. The fans had not been filling the arena. He wanted to change that as soon as possible. So Mark Cuban began to do what he did best—he began to sell. When Mark Cuban was just a child, he made money by selling garbage bags to save up for a new pair of basketball shoes. By the time he was 31, he had sold his first start-up computer business for millions. Then, by his early 40s, he had made billions on his deal with Yahoo.com. So Mark Cuban knew exactly how to sell what his new team had to offer: fun.

Cuban wanted to improve the game experience for the fans. They got free food if the Mavs scored over 100 points, and he also made some of the seats cheaper, so that more people could afford to see the games in person. Cuban also knew that people love to voice their opinions, so he posted

Mark Cuban is just another excited fan during the 2001 playoffs.

Maverick Shawn Bradley dunks the ball during the 2001 playoffs.

his email address on the scoreboard. Fans were encouraged to write him during the game and tell him what they thought. And Cuban took fan suggestions seriously. After getting complaints that not everyone in the arena could see the shot clock, he had a new three-sided shot clock put up. Everyone in the arena could now watch with suspense as the time ticked down.

Mark Cuban also led the fans by example. He came to all the games, and sat in his old seats. He cheered and yelled as loud as ever. But now, instead of being frustrated that his team wasn't winning, Cuban was able to cheer them on to victory after victory. And, it turned out, he would have plenty of company in the stands. Attendance to the home games began to rise. Starting in the second year of Cuban's ownership, all the home games sold out. And they would keep selling out for the next decade.

By the end of the 2000-01 season, it was clear that Mark Cuban was doing something right. The team had won 53 games, and were serious contenders for the first time in a decade. They beat the Utah Jazz in the first round of the playoffs. But they ended up losing to their long-time rivals, the San Antonio Spurs, in the Western Conference Semifinals. But everyone agreed that the Mavericks were now a team to watch. And for Dallas fans, they knew that they had the best show around.

Part-Time Maverick

In another attempt to draw in a crowd, Mark Cuban brought Dennis Rodman to play for the Mavs at the end of the 1999-2000 season. Rodman, however, left after only 12 games.

These Mavs fans dress in their team's colors on the day after Christmas, 2001.

Chapter 4
ALMOST THERE

The new millennium brought with it a lot of great changes for the Dallas Mavericks. With the 1990s behind them, the Mavericks were becoming a very competitive team. Now, losing seasons were a thing of the past. The Mavs were consistent playoff contenders. In 2001, the Mavs moved into a new arena: the American Airlines Center. The whole city was very excited to have a newer, updated arena to replace the old Reunion Arena. In fact, the opening ceremony for this new arena made it into the Guinness Book of World Records for the largest ribbon-cutting ceremony. This new era for the Mavs was definitely a huge improvement over the last decade. However, they still longed to finally become NBA Champions. And while their enthusiastic new owner believed that they could climb to the NBA's mountaintop, the Mavs still had a long road ahead of them.

In 2003, the Mavs reached the Western Conference Finals, and their opponent was the San Antonio Spurs. Dallas's "Big Three" players,

The Dallas skyline with the now familiar American Airlines Center.

The Bulls can't stop Maverick Michael Finley. The crowd stares as Finley takes a shot in this 2003 game.

Dirk Nowitzki, Michael Finley and Steve Nash, steered the Mavs into this series. These players had been around for a number of years. But something had really clicked in the early 2000s, and they were nearly unstoppable. However, during Game 3 against the Spurs, Nowitzki sprained his right knee so badly that he didn't think he could walk. Nowitzki wasn't able to play again in the series, and the Spurs defeated the Mavericks four games to one. It's still up for debate whether the Mavs

Trading for Success

Though Nowitzki had played his entire career with the Mavs, he was originally drafted by the Milwaukee Bucks. He was traded to the Mavs as part of a massive deal that involved four players and three teams.

would have beaten the Spurs had Nowitzki been able to play the rest of the series. But no matter what, it was a huge loss for the team. It had still been a wonderful season for the Mavs, and by many standards, their best season yet.

Then, in 2006, the Mavs found themselves stampeding through the playoffs, but without their "Big Three." Nash had earlier returned to the Phoenix Suns, and Finley left for the Spurs. But Nowitzki still had plenty of very talented company, including guard Jason "The JET" Terry. The Mavs were looking their best. Dallas jumped out to a great start by sweeping the Memphis Grizzlies in the first round. Next, they took on their long-time rivals, the San Antonio Spurs—and their old

teammate Michael Finely. It was a long series—stretching to a deciding Game 7—before the Mavs finally emerged as winners. In the Western Conference Finals they went head-

Nowitzki comes up against old teammate Finley in the second round of the 2006 playoffs.

Smashing Records

The Mavs won 60 games in the regular 2005-06 season. This tied their best-ever season record, and then they went on to beat that record by seven games in the 2006-07 season.

to-head with their old teammate, Steve Nash, and the Phoenix Suns. Once again, the Mavs advanced. And, for the first time in their team history, they were moving on to the Finals.

The whole city of Dallas was in a state of wonder. Their team had finally reached the Finals—and they believed that the Mavs could finish the task. The first two games in the series confirmed this belief. The Mavs defeated the Miami Heat in Games 1 and 2 in Dallas's American Airlines Center. The city was so sure that they would win the rest of the series that they even began to plan a victory parade. And so, when the Mavericks traveled to Miami, there were a lot of expectations, and a lot of pressure.

The Miami arena, also named for American Airlines, was "white hot" for Game 3. The crowd

Confetti and streamers rain down on Dallas fans after the 2006 Game 2 victory against the Heat.

was dressed in their white game shirts, and they, like the Dallas fans, were hoping that their team would win their first ever NBA Championship in 2006. The Heat started off strong, with veteran Shaquille O'Neal powering past the Mavs for a baseline slam dunk. And Miami's Dwyane Wade was playing his best basketball of the series, as he went for 42 points in Game 3. But despite all this, it was a very close contest. Jason Terry kept the Heat on their toes with plenty of jump shots—living up to his nickname of "The JET" by "taking off" and making an 11-foot running jump shot in the middle of the third

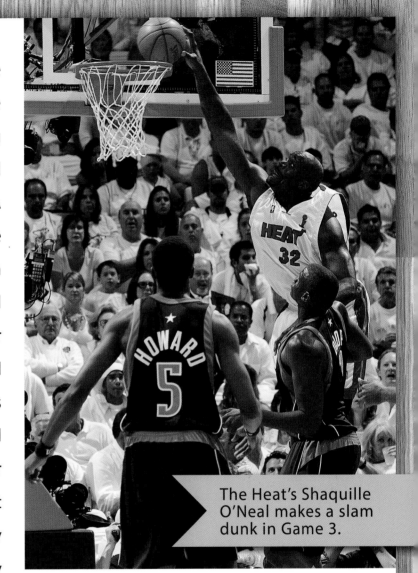

The Heat's Shaquille O'Neal makes a slam dunk in Game 3.

quarter. And Dirk Nowitzki was a constant force on the court. With 15 seconds to go in the fourth quarter, the two teams were tied at 95. That was when Miami's Gary Payton found a hole in the Mavs' defense, and made a clean 21-foot jump shot. This was Payton's only basket of the night. The Heat were up by two.

And now, with only a few seconds remaining in the game, there was a similarly large opportunity for Dirk Nowitzki. He was fouled as he went for an inside layup, and went to the line for two free throws. He made the first, and the Mavs trailed by one. But then, with the whole country watching, Nowitzki missed the tying shot. There was disbelief on the Mavs' faces as the ball bounced off the rim, and into the hands of Dwyane Wade. The Heat won Game 3, and went on to win the following three games,

During Game 3 of the 2006 NBA Finals, Nowitzki misses a free throw in the final seconds of the fourth quarter.

snatching away the Mavs' long-sought-after NBA Championship on Dallas's home court.

Dallas's victory parade was canceled, and the team began to prepare for the next year. Nowitzki gave voice to the pride, and sorrow, that they all felt over the Mavs' first Finals series: "We had a heck of a year. Nobody expected us to come out of the West. But right now, the frustration is high."

But the team was determined that this would not be their last trip to the Finals. And, after five years of very hard work, the Mavs found themselves in almost a mirror image of that 2006 series. They were up against the Heat once more, but this time, the Mavs were leading 3-2. As the Mavs prepared for their trip

The Heat's Dwyane Wade celebrates his team's Game 3 victory of the 2006 NBA Finals.

to Miami, there was one question on everyone's minds—could they return the favor and beat the Heat on Miami's home turf?

A Proud Owner

After the Mavs were defeated in Game 6 of the 2006 Finals, Mark Cuban hugged each player, and thanked them for a wonderful year.

Chapter 5
CHAMPIONS

It was easy to spot the Mavericks' fans in Miami's arena. They were the tiny blue specks surrounded by a blur of white. But for the Dallas players, seeing those patches of blue must have felt like seeing a bit of blue sky emerge from behind the clouds. They could feel their city's love and support, all the way from Texas. The

A Nowitzki fan has fun with the Mavs' slogan.

Mavs had not forgotten about their last trip to the Finals in 2006. And they knew from the shouts of their fans, that they hadn't either. The blue T-shirts up in the crowd read: "The Time is Now." The Mavs had embraced this saying during this season, and they meant to live up to it that night.

Only two of the Mavericks players remained from that 2006 Finals series: Dirk Nowitzki and Jason Terry. But all the Mavs wanted to make up for that bitter loss from

Don't Push Your Luck!
Dallas did not start planning the victory parade for 2011 until after their team won. Many Mavs fans felt that early planning had "jinxed" their shot at the 2006 Championship.

half a decade ago. One player had recently returned to the Mavericks after a 12-year absence. Jason Kidd, one of the "Three Js", had been a bright spot during the '90s. And, at 38 years old, he was still one of the best point guards in the NBA. Kidd had been to the Finals two times with the New Jersey Nets. But he still didn't have a Championship ring. For Nowitzki, Terry, and Kidd— all in their 30s—they didn't know if they would be this close to a championship again.

Game 6 began with determined faces all around. The Mavs felt an

Jason Kidd takes a shot against the Heat's Mario Chalmers in Game 6 of the 2011 NBA Finals.

urgency to finish the series, while the Heat were desperate to hold on for one more game. The Heat's LeBron James put the first points on the board with a 26-foot jump shot, followed closely by a layup. The crowd went wild as James shouldered past the defenders to the basket.

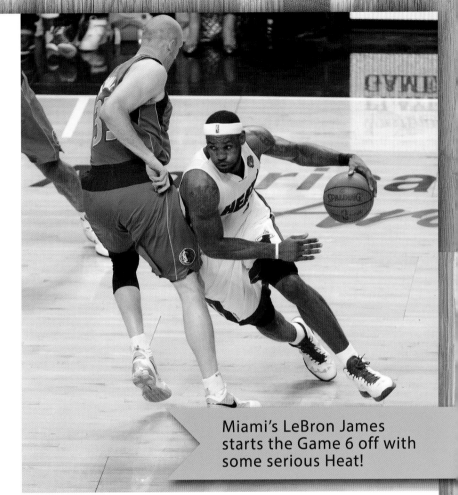

Miami's LeBron James starts the Game 6 off with some serious Heat!

With five minutes left in the first quarter, Jason Terry entered the game. Within a minute, Terry made two jump shots. This new supercharged energy from Jason "The JET" Terry seemed to turn the whole momentum of the game around. The Mavs erased Miami's lead and begain to seize control. Some credit was also due to Jason Kidd, who assisted on three straight

Just a Kidd?

At 38 years old, Jason Kidd became the oldest guard to ever start in an NBA finals game.

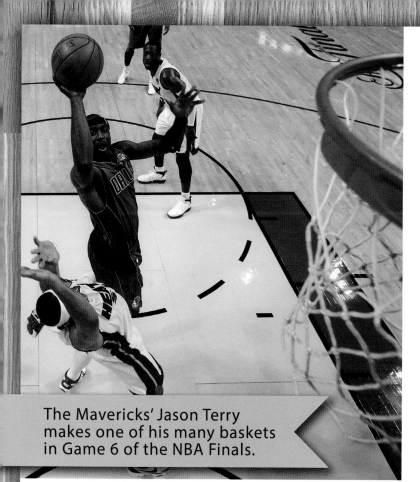

The Mavericks' Jason Terry makes one of his many baskets in Game 6 of the NBA Finals.

The Mavs kept their lead for most of the game. There were a few tense minutes in the middle of the second quarter when the Heat rallied back from a 12-point deficit to take the lead. But, by the end of the fourth quarter, the Mavs had nearly a 10-point lead.

With 2:30 left on the clock, Dirk Nowitzki had the ball, and his path was blocked by the Heat's Chris Bosh. Nowitzki lifted up his long arms to take the shot, only to find Bosh's hands in the way. Dropping the ball back down to his chest, Nowitzki moved with a grace that can only be captured on replay. In slow motion, you could see

baskets in just over a minute. The Mavs led 32-27 at the end of the first quarter.

A Vision of Victory

Jason Terry was so confident that his team would win the 2011 NBA Championship and take home the Larry O'Brien Trophy, that he had a picture of the trophy tattooed on his arm. He got this tattoo in October of 2010, before the season even started.

the way Nowitzki twisted the ball down and across the front of his chest, and into position to take a clear shot. But to the crowd it was a haze of motion—which ended with the ball sinking into the net for another two points. The Heat tried to make up the point differential with a few three-point jump shots, but the Mavs were too far ahead. When the Mavs took Game 6, 105-95, Mark Cuban was there on the sidelines, jumping up and down and yelling with joy.

After 31 long years as a franchise, the Mavs had finally done it. They were the 2011 NBA Champions. And there was no question that they deserved this moment at the top of the NBA's highest peak. The Heat's Chris

Dirk Nowitzki finds a clear shot against the Heat's Chris Bosh.

Mark Cuban watches his team become the 2011 NBA Champions.

Bosh praised the Mavericks for their win: "I think we can take a page out of their book and really just pay attention to people's work ethic and how much time they put into the game." The NBA also gave credit to one particular player for his hard work that season. Dirk Nowitzki was named Finals MVP.

When it came time for the awards ceremony, Mark Cuban had a special request. He asked that the trophy be presented not to himself, but to one of the original owners: Donald

Carter. Cuban waited behind Carter, standing half a head taller than the man in the huge white hat. And beside Donald Carter was his wife, Linda Jo, whose love of basketball had inspired Carter to acquire a basketball team in the first place. The trophy passed from Carter's hands, to Cuban's, and then finally to Nowitzki's—who lifted it high above the entire team. They would return to Dallas as champions. This year they would finally have their parade, and in his typical style, Mark Cuban paid for the entire thing.

In January of 2012, Mark Cuban presented his team—all the players and the coaching staff, with

Championship rings. They stood beneath their Championship banner as Cuban passed out the rings with

Donald and Linda Jo Carter ride with their grandson in the Maverick's victory parade.

Time for a Change?

At first, Mark Cuban didn't want to buy rings for his team. He thought they were too "old school," and wanted something new. But Cuban kept with tradition, and bought his team the traditional rings.

a glittering horse head—their team emblem. Never one to hold back when it came to his team, Cuban had paid $1.4 million for the 15 rings. Though they didn't follow up their 2011 victory with another championship, the 2011-12 season marked the Mavs' 11th straight play-off appearance. Only the Spurs have a longer playoff streak. And, from now on, all home games will be played beneath the Championship banner. Only time will tell how many more banners the franchise will collect. One thing is certain: with their generous owner, and talented players, the Dallas Mavericks have a future as bright as the 2011 rings on their fingers.

Two of the Dallas Mavericks' 2011 NBA Championship Rings.

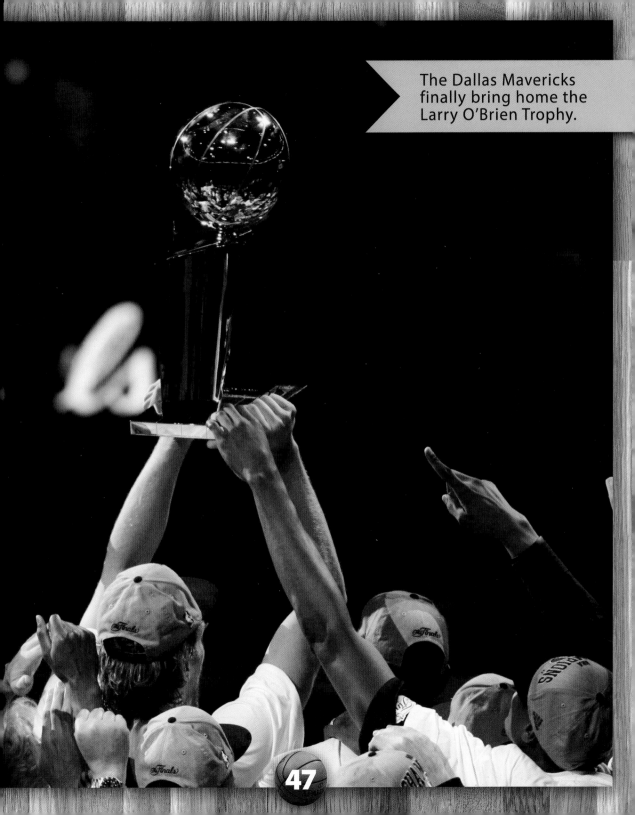

The Dallas Mavericks finally bring home the Larry O'Brien Trophy.